THE BOOK OF
BEARS

by
Andrew Charman

Illustrated by
Chris Forsey

GALLERY BOOKS
An Imprint of W. H. Smith Publishers Inc.
112 Madison Avenue
New York City 10016

CONTENTS

TRUE BEARS

Bears have fascinated and frightened people for centuries. They have been the subject of countless stories, legends and far-fetched tales since people first began to explore the world.

Wild bears are mysterious animals. They live in the great wildernesses of the world. People think that bears are fierce and dangerous, but in fact they are shy, quiet animals. In the past, they have been widely hunted and some have died out. Today, most bears are in danger of dying out if they are not protected. A few are truly endangered animals. Some countries have now put aside large areas where they can be safe.

In this part of the **Book of Bears**, you will find facts about some of the bears which still live in their natural homes. These include the most famous kinds or species: the brown bears and black bears.

SUN BEAR
(Helarctos malayanus)

The sun bear gets its name from the crescent-shaped mark on its chest, which, in eastern folklore, stands for the rising sun. It may also be called this because it loves to sunbathe.

The sun bear is the smallest bear and is only 1.2 metres (4 ft) long when fully grown. It does not make a den in the winter because the tropical forests in which it lives never get very cold. It sleeps during the day and searches for food at night. The sun bear has a varied diet, feeding on rodents, lizards and fruit. It is especially fond of termites. It will dig out a termite nest, insert its forepaws one at a time, and lick off the insects with its very long tongue.

Not very much is known about how the sun bear breeds because it lives in remote places. We do know that the female usually has a litter of two cubs, and that they are born on the forest floor well protected by vegetation.

Tropical bear
The sun bear lives in the tropical and sub-tropical forests of southern Asia.

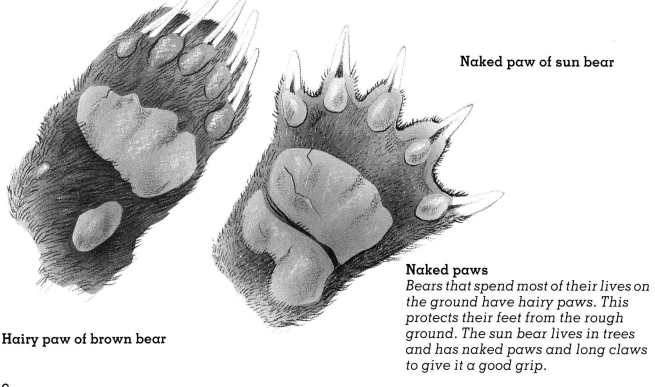

Naked paw of sun bear

Hairy paw of brown bear

Naked paws
Bears that spend most of their lives on the ground have hairy paws. This protects their feet from the rough ground. The sun bear lives in trees and has naked paws and long claws to give it a good grip.

Life in the trees
During the day, the sun bear sleeps or sunbathes in the tops of high trees. At sunset, they become active. Here, two bears show how good they are at balancing on the branch of a tree.

HIMALAYAN BLACK BEAR
(Selenarctos thibetanus)

The Himalayan black bear is easy to recognize because it has a pointed muzzle and a white V-shaped mark on its chest. It is quite small, standing about 1.5 metres (5 ft) high, but is heavy for its size at about 160 kilograms (353lbs). This extra weight is caused by a thick layer of fat beneath the skin, which protects the bear from the cold.

When on the ground and walking, bears move their two right legs together, followed by their two left legs. This is a clumsy-looking shuffle. In fact, bears can run at speeds of up to 19 kilometres an hour (30 mph), which is fast, but not fast enough to catch animals such as deer and antelope. This means that although bears have been described as carnivores (meat-eaters), they have to eat plant food in order to survive. The Himalayan black bear is mainly vegetarian, feeding on berries, roots, nuts, ants and honey, maize, rice and fruit. They have been known to attack cattle, but will take only the young and the sick.

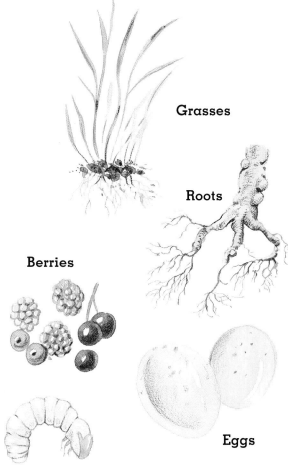

Grasses

Roots

Berries

Grubs

Eggs

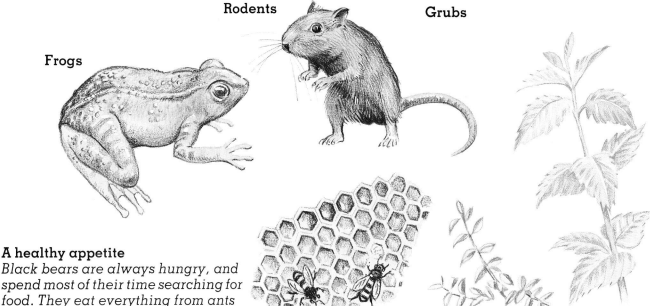

Frogs

Rodents

A healthy appetite
Black bears are always hungry, and spend most of their time searching for food. They eat everything from ants to rice. You can see some of the things that they eat here.

Bees, comb wax, honey

Nettles (and other herbs)

Distant relatives

The Himalayan black bear is a relative of the American black bear, but lives far away from America in the mountains of Kashmir, Nepal, China and Japan. To see one, you don't have to go quite so far, because black bears are the kind most commonly seen in zoos.

EUROPE

ASIA

AFRICA

Sweet-toothed bear

Himalayan black bears are good climbers and have a "sweet tooth." This bear is stealing some bees' honey.

9

AMERICAN BLACK BEAR
(Ursus americanus)

The American black bear is probably the most well-known of the five species of black bear living today. It was once very common, living in nearly all the wooded areas of North America from Central Mexico northwards.

The black bear's fur is shorter than the brown bear's, and comes in a variety of colors from pure black to cinnamon brown. Some even have white patches. They live alone and wander for miles in search of food. They are good climbers and can run at a speed of up to 48 kilometres (30 miles) an hour.

In American National Parks, such as Yellowstone, Wyoming, the black bear is protected and actually increasing in number. Here they are quite used to people. Black bears are known for their playful nature, but they are also very strong. People who visit the parks are asked to stay in their cars for their own protection.

Protected bears
The American black bear once lived all over North America. Today it lives in remote forested places and in the National Parks, where it thrives.

Dozing through the winter

In countries where winter temperatures are very low, some animals hibernate. This is a long winter sleep, during which the animal's body temperature drops, and its breathing slows down. Bears do not hibernate in this sense. Black bears sleep for most of the winter, but they will occasionally emerge during mild spells, perhaps to stretch their legs. Bears eat a lot of food in the fall and build up a thick layer of fat beneath the skin. They live on this during their winter sleep.

EUROPEAN BROWN BEAR
(Ursus arctos)

European brown bears were once very common, roaming the woodlands throughout Europe, and even the dense pine forests of Scotland. Sadly, the last brown bear in Britain was killed in the eleventh century. Today, they can only be found living far away from man, on Europe's wooded mountain slopes.

Bears' diets vary from one animal to another. Only the polar bear is wholly carnivorous, not having much else to eat but meat in its cold, arctic home. Some brown bears eat only meat and others only plant food, but most eat both. They are particularly fond of berries and fruits, insects, small animals, honey and the grubs of wild bees. Fish is also a great favorite, and bears that live close to fast-flowing water will always have this dish on their menu.

Shrinking territories
The areas in which the European brown bear now lives are tiny compared to what they used to be. It lives in mountainous areas of northern Spain, Poland, Germany, Scandinavia and Russia.

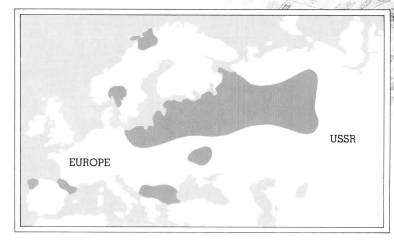

EUROPE

USSR

Secret store
If a brown bear is not desperately hungry, he will bury his catch somewhere and return later. This large brown bear may be taking his fish to a secret hiding place.

GRIZZLY BEAR
(Ursus horribilis)

Adult grizzly bears reach a great size and are very powerful animals. They can grow to about 2 metres (7ft) high at the shoulders and weigh up to 680 kilograms (1,500 lbs).

For most of the year, these bears roam the plains and forests of their natural home alone. They do not live in groups like some other animals. The males and females come together to mate during the summer and then the female goes off on her own to prepare for the birth of her cubs. She builds up a good store of fat during the fall which will help both her and her offspring to survive the long, hard winter.

The mother usually gives birth to two tiny cubs in a den or sheltered cave. When they emerge from their den in spring, the cubs begin their training – learning how to survive in the wild by watching their mother. They play and fight in rough games which teach them about survival. The female grizzly is a good mother, and very strict. If danger threatens she will send her cubs up into a tree, and face the enemy.

Bear of the wilderness
In Canada and Alaska, the grizzly bear lives only in the remote wilderness. In the United States today, it lives in high, lonely areas such as the Rocky Mountains. It is also a resident of the National Parks, such as Yellowstone and Glacier.

Fierce mothers
In spite of its bad reputation, the grizzly bear is not usually harmful to people. However, a mother, or dam, can be very dangerous if she has a family of young cubs to protect. This dam is sniffing the air for danger.

HIMALAYAN BROWN BEAR
(Ursus isabellinus)

The Himalayan brown bear is a very close relative of the European brown bear. It lives in the warmer climate of Central Asia.

Like most bears, the Himalayan brown bear is a wanderer and has a home area or territory of about 16 square kilometres (10 sq. miles). Male bears have a territory to themselves, but the female will share hers with her young cubs. So bears seldom mix with others unless their territories overlap. This often happens if two territories share a rich source of food, such as a river teaming with fish. Visiting bears are rarely challenged. As they are peaceful among themselves, and do not have any enemies in the wild, the hunter with his gun is the creature that bears fear most.

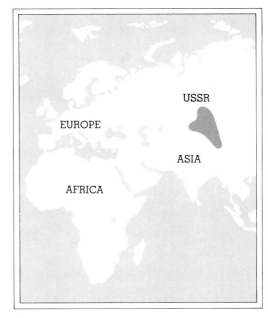

Asian bear
The Himalayan brown bear lives in the mountains of Central Asia. In early summer, it comes down to the plains to eat the young grass.

Making his mark
This bear is marking his territory. Other bears, smelling this scent, will know to stay away.

BLUE BEAR
(Ursus pruinosus)

In spite of its name, the blue bear is related to the brown bears; we say that it is a sub-species of brown bear. It has a blackish-brown coat that is tinged with slate-grey or silver giving it a 'blue' appearance.

There are different sub-species of brown bear all over the world. The European brown bear, the Kodiak bear, the grizzly, the Himalayan brown bear, the Syrian bear and the blue bear all belong to this species. It was once thought that these bears were different species, because there was such a variety of sizes and colors. Today, we believe that they belong to the same species. The color of the coat varies according to the places in which they live. Bears that live in dense forests will have a dark coat because this makes them less easily seen. For the same reason, bears that live in the open and are out in the sun, will have a lighter, silkier coat. Apart from this difference, brown bears are made in much the same way and live similar lives.

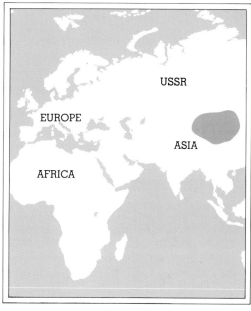

Snow bear
The blue bear, or snow bear, as it is sometimes called, comes from western China and Tibet.

Digging for food
Bears search very thoroughly for their food. They enjoy digging for grubs and roots, and, like this blue bear, they often dig holes much larger than they need to be.

KODIAK BEAR
(Ursus middendorffi)

T he Kodiak bear is the biggest of all the bears and the largest living land carnivore. A fully-grown male standing up on its hind legs can be as tall as 2.7 metres (9 ft), and weigh as much as 748 kilograms (1,650 lbs).

Every year, the adult pink salmon swim upstream to lay their eggs in the inland pools in which they were born. On their way they have to encounter many difficulties, including hungry Kodiak bears. Fish are rich in protein, and it is believed to be this that enables the bears to grow so large.

Kodiak bears are expert fishers. Often they stand on the river bank, reach down and flip the fish from the water with their paws. At other times, they wade into the fast-moving water and snap them up in their powerful jaws.

Down by the river
Kodiak cubs are tiny at birth. They come out of their den at the same time as the salmon are swimming up river. On this rich diet, the cubs grow quickly.

Cold northern home
The Kodiak bear is only found on a group of islands off the Alaskan Peninsula. The largest of these is the Kodiak island.

SYRIAN BEAR
(Ursus syriacus)

The Syrian bear is the smallest brown bear, weighing only 68 kilograms (150 lbs). It is the kind usually seen in European zoos.

For centuries bears have been captured and kept to provide people with entertainment and sport. Until only 70 years ago, it was possible to see dancing bears in market squares and streets of many European towns. These bears were often kept and trained under cruel conditions. Their claws were clipped and their teeth pulled out to make them safe. Today we keep bears in zoos and National Parks for very different reasons. In zoos, they are kept in conditions that match their natural homes as closely as possible. In National Parks, they *are* at home and we travel to them. By studying their physiology (how they are made) and the way they behave, we can understand their needs and perhaps know best how to protect them.

In captivity
It is the Syrian bear that is most often seen in European zoos. In good zoos, they are happy and eat well.

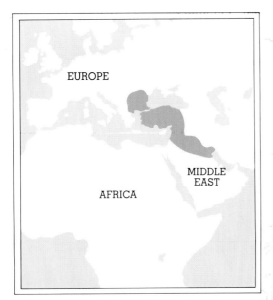

Middle Eastern bear
The Syrian bear comes originally from Syria, but has spread to other countries bordering the Mediterranean Sea.

EUROPE

MIDDLE EAST

AFRICA

ENDANGERED BEARS

Bears live in large territories of forested hills and open plains. When people move in to live in unexplored areas they need lots of space for building and farming.

Bears have always been hunted; for their flesh, for their pelts and because people fear them. With the invention of the gun, hunting became less dangerous and more profitable. For these reasons, many of the bears who once roamed the earth have completely died out – they are extinct. Others are still with us, but are endangered, including the majestic polar bear. In many countries, particularly America, bears are protected. In other parts of the world it may already be too late. You can read about some of the endangered and extinct bears on the following pages.

SLOTH BEAR
(Melursus ursinus)

The sloth bear is now very rare due to the destruction of its natural home, the tropical forest. It does not look like a typical bear because of its long shaggy coat and thick, loose lips. When it was first discovered people thought that they had found a species of sloth, and this is where it gets its name.

Like most bears, the sloth bear is a solitary animal. On hot days it sleeps in a cool cave or den in the depths of the forest. At dawn and dusk it becomes active and starts searching for food. It is very strong and will climb into trees for bird's eggs, fruit and honey. On the ground, it will tear open dead logs and tree-trunks in search of grubs. It is especially fond of ants and termites. It digs a hole into the side of the insects' nest and makes a hole just big enough for its muzzle. Then it makes a funnel with its lips, blows away the dust and sucks up its dinner. The funny noise that this makes can be heard a long way away.

A free ride
Female sloth bears give birth to two cubs in the safety of their den. When they emerge, 2 or 3 months later, they stay with their mother, and ride on her back by clinging to the long hair between her shoulders.

Indian bear
The sloth bear lives in the forests of India and Sri Lanka, where the population is now increasing. In 1975 it was estimated that there were about 8,000 bears.

EUROPE

ASIA

AFRICA

POLAR BEAR
(Tharlarctos maritimus)

The polar bear is the largest and strongest land animal to be found in the Arctic. Adults can grow up to 2.7 metres (9 ft) long and weigh as much as half a tonne (0.5 ton). In spite of their size, they are very agile and their limbs are very powerful. Thick fur on the soles of their broad feet enables them to jump and run on the slippery ice, and protects them from frost. The polar bear's fur is white all year round. In summer it becomes yellower to match the color of the melting snow. The polar bear has two kinds of fur; close to the skin is a dense underfur to keep the body warm, and outside this are longer guard hairs for added protection.

For the long winter period, which lasts nearly nine months, the male polar bear is a solitary hunter. It will wander for miles in search of food. In the spring, the female polar bears take their cubs along, showing them how to catch food for themselves.

An expert hunter
The favorite food of polar bears is ringed seals. Here, an adult bear is stalking her prey, closely followed by two young cubs. It is said that a stalking bear will hide its black nose by raising a paw to its face.

Arctic dweller

Polar bears live along the southern edge of the Arctic pack ice. In recent years, measures have been taken to protect the polar bears. In 1981 there were 20,000 bears in the Arctic.

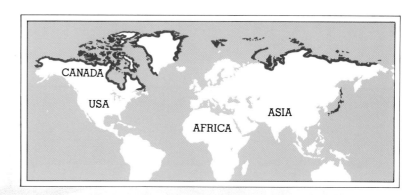

Safe and warm

When winter comes, the female bear digs into a bank of snow and ice to make her den. Here the cubs are born, safe from predators and the harsh weather outside. They stay with their mother for most of the winter feeding on her milk.

Flat-footed bear
Bears' legs are jointed like ours. You can see from this picture that bears walk the way we do, placing the whole of the foot on the ground. Animals that walk this way are called plantigrades. Dogs, on the other hand, walk on their toes, and are called digitigrades.

Taking to the water
Polar bears are sometimes forced to swim. They swim strongly, using only their front legs. The thick layer of fat beneath their skin helps them to stay afloat and keeps out the cold.

SPECTACLED BEAR
(Tremarctos ornatus)

This small bear, weighing from 65kg (143lbs) to 135kg (286lbs), gets its name from the white marks around its eyes. These sometimes look like a pair of glasses or spectacles. It has a shaggy black coat, but the coat is not as thick as that of bears which live in colder regions of the world.

The spectacled bear is an expert climber and will search for food in the highest branches of very tall trees. Like the sun bear (see page 6), it may build a nest of sticks, on which it sleeps during the day.

We do not know very much about the everyday life of this bear, because it lives in dense tropical forests far away from man. We do know that it feeds mainly on leaves, fruit and roots, although it will sometimes eat meat. One large male bear which lived for many years in the New York Zoological Park, was very fond of milk, apples and raisin bread.

Bear of the southern hemisphere
The spectacled bear lives in South America. The numbers of these bears had dwindled so much that conservation areas have recently been set aside for them. In Ecuador, there are now thought to be about 8,000 bears.

ATLAS BEAR
(Ursus crowtheri)

The Atlas bear, or brown Atlas bear as it was known, once lived in North Africa. It is the only bear ever to have lived in this part of the world. It was a thickset, stout bear, with a pointed black muzzle and long shaggy fur. It is said to have been very unlike other bears, with much shorter toes and claws.

From the writings of the Ancient Romans, we learn that the Atlas bear was common 2,000 years ago. Long before that time, North Africa was densely forested, and provided ideal bear territory. The Romans cleared the forests for timber, and so began a process that has left much of this area as desert. The bears retreated to the mountains of Morocco and Algeria. When the gun was introduced, the number of bears decreased even more. It is believed that some were still alive in 1867, but they are certainly extinct now.

African bear
The Atlas bear lived in North Africa, at that time a densely forested area. Later it ventured into the mountains of Morocco and Algeria.

EUROPE

AFRICA

The hunter
*The Atlas bear and its natural home,
as shown here, have both disappeared.
Here an adult bear chases an onager,
an animal that is also extinct.*

MEXICAN SILVER GRIZZLY BEAR
(Ursus nelsoni)

The Mexican silver grizzly was a member of the brown bear species and was very closely related to the grizzly that still exists today. It was the largest native animal of Mexico, being 183 centimetres (6 ft) long and weighing up to 318 kilograms (700 lbs).

When the Spanish first explored Mexico and America in 1540, this was the bear they met. They called it 'el oso plateado' meaning 'the silver one'. At that time, the bears' homelands covered the whole of the western half of North America including the Rocky Mountains. But the silver grizzly's story is not a happy one. It was hunted so much for its beautiful fur that by the 1930s it could only be found in the isolated mountains of the state of Chihuahua. In 1960, a concerted effort by rangers to track down the remaining bears was so successful that by 1964 the silver grizzly was extinct.

Prized for its pelt
The Mexican silver grizzly had a fur quite unlike that of any bear living today. It was highly prized by hunters.

Mexican grizzly
In 1540, when Europeans first colonized America, the silver grizzly occupied the western part of North America and Mexico.

CANADA

USA

MEXICO ▶

SOUTH
AMERICA

KAMCHATKAN BEAR
(Ursus piscator)

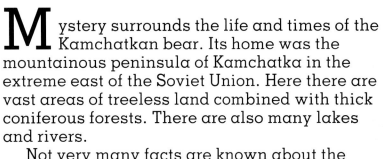

Mystery surrounds the life and times of the Kamchatkan bear. Its home was the mountainous peninsula of Kamchatka in the extreme east of the Soviet Union. Here there are vast areas of treeless land combined with thick coniferous forests. There are also many lakes and rivers.

Not very many facts are known about the Kamchatkan bear, but there are many stories and legends. It was a large, heavy bear. Russian hunters recorded weights of between 653 kilograms (1,441 lbs) and 685 kilograms (1,510 lbs). This is almost as large as the biggest of the Kodiak and polar bears which still live today. The largest Kamchatkan bears had very beautiful short, pure-black coats. They were probably hunted for their skins or pelts. We do not know exactly what caused their extinction, but it seems certain that there were no bears remaining in this isolated part of the world after 1920.

Fast-water fishers
The rivers of Kamchatka are rich hunting places for bears. Like their cousins, the grizzly and the Kodiak bears, Kamchatkan bears were expert fishers.

Bears and volcanoes

The Kamchatka peninsula, once the home of this brown bear, is between the Bering Sea and the Sea of Okhotsk. It is 1,200 kilometres (746 miles) long and has 20 active volcanoes.

USSR

ALASKA

BERING SEA

SEA
OF
OKHOTSK

CAVE BEAR
(Ursus spelaeus)

The ancestors of the bears that we see today lived 26 million years ago. They belonged to an animal family that included dogs and wolves, but instead of living only on meat, the bears' diet gradually changed to include fruit and vegetation. They developed teeth for crushing and chewing tough plant food.

The earliest bears were like small black bears, but were replaced by the kind found today, and another type called the cave bear. This bear lived during the Ice Ages and was around at the same time as our own distant ancestors. It was almost completely vegetarian and only visited caves for its winter sleep. Many bears died during the winter, and one cave in Austria contains the remains of 30,000 bears.

The bears spread to North America 500,000 years ago. The cave bear seems to have become extinct before the end of the Ice Age, about 15,000 years ago.

The first bear-hunters
The cave bear was taller than a Kodiak bear and must have seemed very fierce. Our ancestors probably killed the bears for food, and for their fur, which would have been ideal for keeping out the cold.

35

Competing for caves

About 30,000 years ago, man and bear competed for the best form of natural shelter: the cave. The bears slept in the caves during the winter. They may also have hidden in caves to escape from hunters.

BARELY BEARS

Bears have always lived in places that are far away from man and difficult to explore. When people started naming animals and putting them into groups, they sometimes made mistakes. They were often confused by animals which looked like bears, such as the panda. We now think that the panda belongs to a different group of animals.

Other animals, such as the koala, are known to belong to completely different groups but are still called bears because of their striking similarity to the real thing. You can read about these animals in this part of the book. Finally, teddy bears look just like the real thing, because they were originally modelled on a living bear. You can read all about the first teddy, and of those that followed it, in this section too.

KOALA
(Phascolarctos cinereus)

The koala is probably Australia's favorite animal. Although it looks like a bear, with its thick fur and stumpy tail, the koala belongs to a family of animals called marsupials.

Koalas live alone or in small groups, and spend nearly all of their time in trees. They climb in a series of small jumps, gripping onto the tree trunk with their powerful claws. During the day, koalas sleep in the fork of a tree. At night, they feed in the highest branches of their trees. They eat only the youngest most tender shoots of one kind of tree, the eucalyptus. The leaves of this tree are so moist that koalas rarely need to drink water.

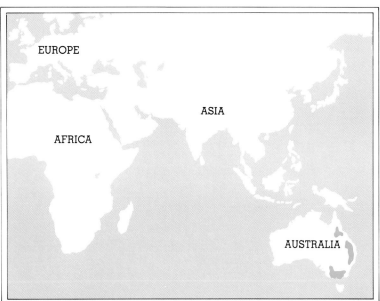

Saving the koala
In the past, koalas were widely hunted. Today they are protected in nature reserves. It is not easy to look after koalas, because they are fussy eaters. In parts of Australia they do, however, thrive in their thousands.

Babe in a pouch

The koala belongs to a group of animals called marsupials. Females of these kinds of animals have special pouches on their bodies. When the baby koala is born it crawls through its mother's fur and climbs into this pouch. Here it feeds on her milk for about 6 months. After that, it comes out of the pouch and rides piggy-back until it is old enough to look after itself.

GIANT PANDA
(Ailuropoda melanoleuca)

The giant panda lives high up in the cold and damp bamboo forests of China. The Chinese call it 'beishung', meaning 'white bear'. When it was first discovered by western scientists in 1869, nobody was really sure whether to call it a bear or raccoon, because the two kinds of animal are very similar in many ways. To solve the problem, they put the panda in a family of its own.

The panda is stockily built with a body nearly 2 metres (6 ft) long, and a stumpy tail. It spends most of its time on the ground, but can climb trees quite well, if a bit clumsily, when chased by predators. Not very much is known about how the panda lives, because it is a shy animal and lives in remote places. We do know that they live alone, except during the mating season, and that they do not sleep throughout the winter. They mate in the spring and two cubs are born the following January. The female feeds her young sitting up and cradling them in her arms rather like human mothers.

Tree-top look-out
Pandas climb very well, even when fully grown. This panda has found a safe and comfortable perch high up in a fir tree.

Bear of the high country

The giant panda lives on the bamboo-covered hillsides of eastern Tibet and Szechwan in southeast China. They thrive in these cool regions which are between 1,500 and 4,000 metres (5,000 and 13,000 ft) above sea level.

A big eater

The panda has five clawed toes on each foot. On each forefoot it has a small pad. This acts as a thumb for grasping bamboo shoots which are its favorite food. It also eats other plants as well as small animals. The panda has a big appetite and eats for 10 – 12 hours a day.

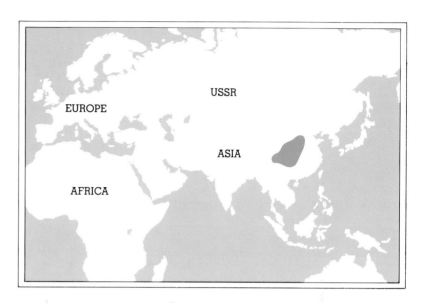

Zoo favorite

The panda is thought to be rare in its native continent. For this reason it is important that they breed in zoos. Pandas are great favourites in zoos, where they love to play and amuse people with their acrobatics.

CAT-BEAR
(Ailurus fulgens)

The cat-bear is the original panda. In Nepal, where this animal lives, it is known as 'Nyalyaponga'. The first explorer to bring one to Europe shortened this to 'panda'. Nowadays, it is sometimes called the red panda so as not to be confused with the giant panda. The cat-bear spends most of its time in the trees. It sleeps by day curled up on its side on a branch or in the hollow of a tree. Early in the morning and in the evening it forages for food, on the ground.

Once out of the trees, it is a clumsy walker and it is a bit pigeon-toed. It eats leaves, fruit, acorns and eggs, and has been known to raid human villages for a taste of milk and butter. It is a peaceful animal but if frightened, the cat-bear will hiss and lash out with its long sharp claws.

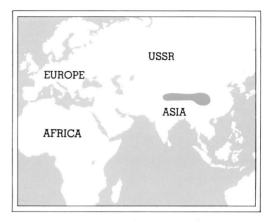

Bear of the mountain trees
The cat-bear lives in mountain forests and bamboo thickets from Nepal to western China. Its home is between 2,120 and 3,640 metres (7,000 and 12,000 ft) above sea level.

Long-tailed jumper
When it jumps from tree to tree, the cat-bear uses its long tail to balance its body.

TEDDY BEAR

I n 1902, Theodore (Teddy) Roosevelt, naturalist and the president of the United States of America, captured a black bear cub while out hunting. He could not bring himself to part with the animal and brought him home as a pet. A doll maker from Brooklyn, named Morris Michtom, used this bear as a model for a doll and with the permission of its owner called it the Teddy bear.

The Teddy bear's popularity was immediate and worldwide. Today they come in all shapes, sizes and colors. Unlike true bears, teddy bears are very sociable and do not make dens in the winter. In other ways they are very similar to their cousins in the wild. They live up to the reputation bears have for being playful, enjoy the company of humans and like sweet things to eat.

Many teddy bears have become stars of the stage, films and television. These include such famous bears as Winnie-the-Pooh, Paddington and Super Ted.

Teddy bears' picnic
Teddy bears enjoy a good picnic. These events always take place in sunny glades. There is music and dancing, and honey served – with everything.

INDEX